Introducing Guinea Pigs

After the dog, cat and rabbit, the guinea pig is possibly the most popular pet mammal. It has many virtues and few, if any, vices. These handy-sized little rodents have been kept under captive conditions for hundreds of years. Their origins are the forests and grasslands of South America. The Incas are known to have bred guinea pigs as a source of food. They are also known as cavies, either name being correct, this deriving from their scientific name of *Cavia asperea*. Actually, no one knows from which of the numerous wild cavies our domesticated pet was evolved, as the process was commenced so long ago.

The Spanish conquistadors introduced the guinea pig to Europe during the 16th century. They were returning from the New World countries, including Guyana, and as the cavy looked somewhat like a pig it is possible that these facts resulted in the name guinea pig. Whatever the truth, the reality was that these little animals adapted well to the temperate

A SAVE-OUR-PLANET BOOK
THE PROFITS GO TO CONSERVATION

GUINEA PIGS
... as a hobby

CONTENTS

Photography: Isabelle Francais, Michael Gilroy, Susan C. Miller, Brian Seed, Vincent Serbin, and Sally Anne Thompson

©TFH 1991

TFH Publications, Inc.,
Neptune, N.J. 07753 USA

TFH Publications, The Spinney, Parklands, Denmead, Portsmouth, PO7 6AR, England

Guinea pigs are scientifically known as *Cavia asperea* and that is where their common name *cavies* originates. Cavies are a worldwide favorite for pet and laboratory animals.

climate and soon became popular pets with those who could afford them. Today, the guinea pig is known all over the world and, by selective breeding and the retention of natural mutations, there are now over 40 varieties that you can choose from.

Guinea pigs are excellent as pets for children. The child must be instructed in the proper care of the guinea pig. This care involves grooming (below) and holding (bottom facing page). It is an adult's responsibility to train their children in guinea pig care.

They make ideal companions for rabbits, and their care and needs are much the same. They are rather more timid than rabbits, and a good bit more nimble. There is not the difference in sizes in cavies as is seen in rabbits, so none are going to grow to a size you did not expect. Guinea pigs enjoy a tremendous following as exhibition animals—adults as well as children breed them as a hobby.

Guinea pigs are available in many colors and coat types. Usually their physical characteristics have little to do with their quality as a pet. There may be, however, personality problems between the animal and the child, especially if the child is rough with the animal.

Unlike rabbits, guinea pigs are not prolific breeders in terms of their litter sizes, so you will not be confronted with an excess of stock that is difficult to sell or give away.

Another difference between these two popular pets is that the babies of a guinea pig are born fully furred and with their eyes open. They are running around and able to feed within hours of their birth. They are not as long lived as rabbits, but many will live well past their sixth year. Sows may still be breeding

purchase and keep, are very amusing and inquisitive, and possess an interesting range of vocal calls. In the following chapters all of their basic needs

when three or more years of age, boars somewhat longer.

All in all, the guinea pig is a delightful little pet. They rarely bite (unless badly handled), are inexpensive to

are detailed so you can enjoy them to the fullest measure.

The child to the right is holding her pet guinea pig correctly. In this grip the cavy cannot wriggle free and fall. The same is not true for the child on the left. She has no control over the security of the cavy.

Accommodation

Any hutch suitable for a rabbit will be just fine for your guinea pig. The important points to consider when buying or making a hutch are that it is as roomy as possible, is constructed of durable materials, is water and damp proof, and is so made that it can be cleaned easily. It will be somewhat less costly to produce a hutch that will be kept indoors than one that must endure the rigors of

A suitable hutch for your cavy or guinea pig must be easily cleaned and taken apart.

inclement winters. Most people house guinea pigs in sheds or similar outbuildings, but we have kept many in outdoor situations and they have coped well enough with the rigors of a northerly climate—but their accommodation was designed with this in mind.

If the hutch can't be taken apart, the hutch must be small enough for someone to get inside to thoroughly clean it.

Hutch Size and Materials

A reasonable size for a guinea pig hutch would be about 76x38x38cm (30x15x15in). This would be roomy without being too generous, so if possible make the length and width larger, especially if two or more cavies are to be housed. Keeping a single guinea pig is not recommended because they really do need company. If it is planned to keep rabbits as well, then the depth and height should be increased a few inches.

The timber used for construction should be 1.25cm (1/2in) thick for the sides, back and roof, with the base being 1.88cm (3/4in). The panels can then be mounted onto a frame made of 5x5cm (2x2in) timber. The roof should be sloped to take away rainwater, and it should overhang all walls to provide

keeps its shape. It costs more but will last a lot longer. If the hole size is larger than that given, this will allow unwanted critters to get in—mice, rats and maybe snakes. If the weldwire is painted with black bitumen paint, this will make it less visible thus better to see in. You can also purchase plastic-coated weldwire.

place by swivel latches and wooden struts. It is useful to feature a tough clear plastic strip behind the viewing panels and doors so that when these are opened the guinea pigs are not at risk of falling out.

Guinea pigs can easily be kept in a small cage. The boy is attaching a water bottle to the guinea pig cage. The water need not be changed daily if you use a special demand water bottle.

protection. It can be covered with roofing felt to ensure it is really waterproof.

The front viewing panel should feature 2.5x2.5cm weldwire, which looks better than chicken wire and

The weldwire can either be placed onto a wooden door frame that swings up, sideways or down, or it can be a frame that can be removed entirely at cleaning times, and held in

Such a panel need only be a few inches tall and can slide into position via grooves at either side of the door.

Many breeders feature sliding trays in their hutches to facilitate easier cleaning, and these are best made of plastic or aluminum. However, they are not essential and if you have applied a number of coats of paint to the hutch floor this, together with a base of sawdust, should protect the wood from urine soaking into it. The entire hutch should be well painted or treated with a suitable preservative. Whether outdoors or in a building, it is best to have your hutch raised off the ground. This will allow air to circulate under the floor, reduce the risk of draft into the hutch, and will make viewing the guinea pigs easier—no need to bend over.

If you plan to breed, you can have some hutches of smaller dimensions and they can be built in tiers. It is best if you construct them such that they have removable siding panels inserted so these can be removed if required to create larger units. If you do breed your pets, try to provide a good exercise area for them to run about in. This is easily provided via an open pen indoors, or a

covered one if outside.

You could also have a large rectangular pen that could be moved from one place to another so the guinea pigs can browse on the grass without overgrazing it. The floor of such a unit can be covered with weldwire, and it could contain a little den for them to go in if it rained or was very hot. Such a unit would protect them from cats and dogs if you were not around at the time.

Many cages are portable. They can be used as a permanent mobile home for your cavies. Petshops have many carriers, especially those made for dogs or cats, which are also suitable for cavies or guinea pigs.

Hutch Design

The conventional shape of a hutch is a rectangle, but if you have the space it could be circular, though such a shape is obviously more difficult to construct. It will ideally contain at least two compartments. One is the sleeping area, and the other is the living area. Place a communicating hole or sliding door at the back end of the hutch so it minimizes draft. You could add a separate toilet area on the other side of the living space and the cavies will use this, which will reduce the fecal matter and urine in the living/feeding area. Guinea pigs are very clean animals and prefer not to unduly foul their living or sleeping quarters.

Cages or hutches can be as elaborate or practical as necessary.
Essentially the hutch must keep the pet in and everything else out! This cage is periodically moved so the ground stays fresh (from waste droppings) and the grass grows as a fresh food for the cavies.

This is a fairly elaborate hutch. It is constructed of outdoor type wood; the bolts are rustproof. Since your cavy may be kept outdoors all year, it enjoys an occasional romp in the snow and munching on fresh grass.

If you have an enclosure for the guinea pigs to run in, this can contain rocks, logs and earthenware sewage pipes. Guinea pigs enjoy playing, and the pipes provide them with somewhere to hide in if something startles them. You can have a grassed area and this they will happily browse on. There really is no limit to the design possibilities of an attractive and functional home for your pets. The more room you give them the more interesting you will find them to be.

Floor and Bedding Material

The best floor material is sawdust, as it absorbs urine very well. Check that it is from woods not treated with chemicals. Wood shavings are good but not as absorbent. Straw is a poor covering, of little nutritional value, and can damage your pet's eyes if a sharp piece were to catch these. Shredded paper is fine but soon looks messy, though it is warm and snug for the sleeping area floor. Granulated paper is a better option for the living area but is more expensive.

Wood shavings are acceptable as an absorbent floor material if the shavings are from soft wood. Sawdust is the best flooring material because it is so absorbent.

Guinea pigs require a secure place in which they can hide. It need not be fancy...a large flowerpot will do.

Your pets should be transported in a safe, comfortable manner. A box such as this one is ideal for transporting your guinea pigs. Note the ventilation holes on the side panel.

One great characteristic of guinea pigs is their friendliness. They don't discriminate. If they like children, they like ALL children. They make wonderful pets for schools.

For the bedroom, hay is undoubtedly your best choice. It is warm, soft and a very good food. Be sure it is fresh smelling, and contains no mold. Meadow hay is the best as it contains clover, dandelion and other wild plants the guinea pigs will enjoy eating. It will of course need replacing every two or three days as your pets eat it. Place a bundle in the sleeping area, and the guinea pigs will soon make a nice nest of it.

Guinea pigs are especially prone to health problems caused by damp weather so be real sure an outside hutch is protected from rain. In an outbuilding no heat will be required, though you might appreciate some when you are attending to chores. It will also be useful if you obtain an ionizer, which can be plugged into a light socket. This will keep the air clear of much dust and bacteria. Bird and pet stores may sell them, if not they are available via specialty bird suppliers in particular. They are popular in birdrooms that have similar problems.

Guinea pigs are one of Nature's environmental favorites. They chew up lawn clippings and their droppings are biodegradable and excellent fertilizer.

Feeding Dishes

Choose heavy pot dishes, as these will not so easily be toppled over. You will want one for dry foods and one for softfood and mashes. By placing softfoods (fruits, etc.) in a dish, this will reduce the amount of sawdust that clings to it—though often the guinea pigs will take it from the dish and promptly drop it on the floor!

Petshops sell lots of drinking water and feeding dishes for pets. It is NOT advised to use plastic dishes. They are too light and easily tip from the movements of the cavy. They are also chewable...at least a guinea pig (cavy) thinks so.

Water is best given by an automatic dispenser. These are inverted bottles with a tube from them. The guinea pig licks the tube and this pushes a ball bearing up and thus releases water. In cold weather the bottle must be checked daily because although the water may not freeze the little ball bearing might get frozen into position—so it does not operate as it should.

The hutch should be routinely cleaned daily. Once a week it should receive a full

Your local pet supplier can offer you heavy crock or pot dishes for your guinea pig. Be sure to get a water dispenser, too.

Guinea pigs can beg like dogs! Be sure that all leafy vegetables or grass have been washed free of insecticides and fertilizers.

clean out and wash so you greatly reduce the risk of parasitic or bacterial invasion and subsequent health risks. If strong disinfectants are used be sure to give the hutch a good washing down with water to remove any excess disinfectant, which can cause irritation to these little pets.

Choosing a Guinea Pig

The factors you will be considering when choosing a guinea pig will be age, variety, health and where to obtain your pets. Health is the most important because without it the other aspects may have little value.

You can guess the age of a guinea pig by its size. The smaller the pig, the younger is it. With adults, it's more difficult. In any case, handle the guinea pig before you buy it to be sure it is tame and accustomed to human handling.

Age

Guinea pigs are weaned from their mother's milk by the time they are about 4-5 weeks of age and this is the best time to obtain them in order to make them really nice pets. If they are a week or two older this is not a problem; indeed they will be that little bit more established. They must be handled a lot, and very gently, if they are to overcome their natural timidity.

Try to buy a cavy about one month old. Then, with lots of love, affection and handling, they become lovable pets. If you intend to breed them, start out with the same colors, though this is no guarantee that the babies will be true-to-color.

Different colors and shades are constantly being developed in cavies. Select the color that appeals to you.

Do remember they are nimble so be sure you have a secure hold of them when lifting them up or they might jump from you and damage their little legs. Secure the pet under its chest, with its legs either side of your fingers, whilst holding the neck and back with your free hand. Instruct children carefully on how to hold their pets.

If you are going to keep your cavy in an area in which he will be viewed from above, consider getting a guinea pig which is visually attractive when viewed from above, such as this American crested red.

Never hold your guinea pig in one hand like this! Hold it under its chest with its legs dangling. Use two hands.

Exhibition and breeding stock are perhaps best obtained when they are at least 5-6 months of age. Before this time it will not have developed well enough for you to assess its potential, or rather for the breeder to have done this for you. Although cavies are sexually mature by this time, they are not physically fully grown until they are 12-15 months of age. However, a sow should be bred from before she is 6-7 months of age; otherwise, she might have problems with her first birth due to her hip bones becoming rather tight set.

If you start a breeding program be warned! Children love pets and when they raise them from birth, they might not want to give them up.

If you are interested in showing your guinea pigs in a competition, you must start with young stock not more than 6 months old. The breeders should be of known parentage. Stock younger than 6 months might not show the characteristics by which they are judged. Here are an old and young specimen of the same basic breed. The difference between these two specimens is obvious.

Variety

A number of varieties are described in the final chapter so here it can be said that for first-time owners it is best to stick with one of the selfs or the Abyssinian. The Peruvian variety has a very long coat and this requires much attention. It soon gets messed up in the average hutch. This variety you can progress to once you have gained experience and if you like shaggy coated guinea pigs.

This tri-colored Abyssinian guinea pig is fine quality and is kept that way by constant grooming.

Solid colored guinea pigs, or cavies, are called *self colored*. The photo above shows two mature self reds. Younger self reds are darker.

There is no shortage of crossbred guinea pigs, but as they cost as much to feed and care for, and as guinea pigs are inexpensive pets, you may as well obtain a pet of a recognized variety. It does not matter which sex you obtain, but do not keep two boars together as they will fight. Sows are fine with each other, and a boar can be kept with its own harem of sows without problem.

Health

If you apply common sense, it is not difficult to select a healthy youngster. You may not be able to assess its quality, but you need no experience to tell if an animal is not as it should be. Firstly, look at the conditions under which it is kept. If these are cramped, damp, dirty or in any way not satisfactory to you, then walk away because the chances are the stock may be harboring a problem even if it is not showing signs of it at that moment. The same applies if you see one member of a litter or group that is clearly unwell—again chances are the others may have contracted the problem. The unwell specimen should have been removed by the seller for attention.

The two cavies shown on these pages LOOK healthy. The eyes, alertness, fur and feet (clean claws) plus their general appearance almost guarantees they are as healthy as you can get without a veterinarian's examination of their stool and blood.

Observe the guinea pigs as they move around. They should show no signs of impediment whatsoever. They are very fast when they are little. Select one or two for inspection. The eyes should be round and clear, with no evidence of staining or weeping. The nose should be dry, with neither nostril in any way swollen or clogged. The ears are tiny and slightly crinkled. The incisor teeth of the upper jaw should fit neatly over those of the lower jaw. If they are not correctly aligned, this could result in eating problems and the teeth growing up or down into the jaw. They can be trimmed by your vet, but such stock is unsuited to breeding and undesirable in a pet.

In order to judge the health of your pet, you should remember what his nose looks like. These three cavies have different nasal appearances. The guinea pig above has a nose covered with hair. It is healthy as long as the hair is dry. The cavy below is ill as its nose is wet, shiny, discolored and has a discharge. The cavy on the facing page has a healthy nose but it is neither bald like the sick cavy, nor covered.

The body should be supple, with no bald areas or signs of fleas and their like. Brush the fur against its lie to see the skin is clean and free from flea dirt. Guinea pigs are especially susceptible to invasion by small mites, so do give the skin and fur scrutiny.

The legs are small and should be complete, including the tiny nails. There are four toes on the front feet and three on the back. However, sometimes a fourth toe is found on the rear foot. This will in no way impede the guinea pig, but it is undesirable.

The perfect head of a healthy cavy. Note that the nose is completely covered with dry, clean fur. The hair is neat and uniform all over the body. The claws are neat and clean, too.

A genetic defect manifested by an extra toe on each of the two rear feet.

The anal region should be clean with no evidence of staining or dried fecal matter around it. Look at the feces in the youngster's cage or pen. This should be like small pellets—firm and not liquid. Any bloodstained droppings is a bad sign.

You can look at this guinea pig and just wonder if it has fleas because every other sign shows it to be very healthy! It should have four claws on the front feet and three on the back feet, not like the cavy on the facing page which has four claws on its rear feet. Its hair is clean, neat and the animal is clean. The supple body is manifested when the cavy moves about.

Where to Buy

Petshops often have a range of guinea pigs in stock at reasonable prices. They may not all be purebred but should be sound healthy little pets. If you want a particular variety, maybe to exhibit or breed, then you must seek out a reputable breeder whose stock you can see. The best place to contact such people is at a local show, or via the local guinea pig club. At a show you will see lots of varieties and can soon strike up a conversation with a number of breeders. You may have to wait awhile for certain varieties that are not bred on a large scale. If you are looking for a particular color, then do not rush matters—patience is definitely a virtue when buying any livestock.

The best place to buy a guinea pig or cavy as it is called in some places, is your local petshop. The main reason is that the petshop has all the supplies and will always be there to help you. They also have a legal responsibility in most places to supply a healthy animal or give you a refund or exchange if it becomes ill within a short period of time after you purchased it.

Above: A golden satin which won *Best in Rare Breed* at the Greater London Cavy Show. Below, pet quality cavies, all pregnant. Can you see the difference between a champion and a pet quality animal?

Feeding

The guinea pig, like the rabbit, is a herbivore. This means its diet is composed of vegetable matter in its many forms. Your pet will therefore eat the same foods as a rabbit. There is one important aspect with guinea pigs that should never be overlooked. Apart from the primates (monkeys, apes and man), it is the only known mammal that cannot synthesize vitamin C in its body. This means it must be provided in the diet.

Guinea pigs only eat vegetable matter, though they have been known to occasionally chew on dried out insects. Offer it scrap vegetables including raw, cooked and those which are tinned or canned, but not vegetables which have been pickled.

Longhaired guinea pigs are beautiful to look at but require a lot of attention to keep their fur in a presentable condition. They are not recommended for the beginner.

This vitamin is found in many foods such as greens, grasses, turnip tops, carrots, berries, melons, oranges and other fruits, wild plants and potatoes.

As long as you supply a varied diet the guinea pig will obtain its needed rations. It can also be supplied via a powder, or tablet. These must be stored in a cool dark place, as the vitamin is especially unstable and is quickly destroyed by light and increased temperatures—so it is largely lost if foods are boiled.

Typical Foods

The guinea pig is really easy to cater for because much of its diet can be supplied from items you will already have in your kitchen. The diet can be divided into two basic parts, which are dryfoods and softfoods. The former comprise oats, bran, maize and wheat together with all products made from these. These will include stale (not moldy) bread, toast, cookies (but not too many sweet ones), pastry and crackers. Cavies will also enjoy certain nuts (shelled), and they relish things such as cheese and scrambled egg (in limited quantity), and mashes that are made up of a mixture of all of these. You can also add a few rabbit pellets, which contain concentrated foods, but do not feed too many of these. You can purchase bags of ready-mixed guinea pig foods from your petshop.

Guinea pig rations are either dried or naturally soft. The dried foods should always be available in a heavy crock dish. The soft foods, like lettuce, should be changed daily. Cooked or raw carrots are also relished and should be offered regularly.

Softfoods broadly cover all plants, vegetables and fruits that contain a high liquid content. Examples are thus apples, strawberries, oranges, pineapple, tomato, berries, beets, potatoes, broccoli, celery and grasses, especially hay. Wild plants include clover, dandelion, chickweed, yarrow, groundsel, indeed most wild plants as long as you avoid poisonous ones. The latter include any plants grown from bulbs, buttercups, deadly nightshade, hemlock and lily of the valley to name but a few. Fortunately, guinea pigs will reject dangerous plants and the little bit that might be eaten will usually be countered by the beneficial plants.

Your pets will enjoy the leaves of many flowers, such as roses, daisies, marigolds and sunflowers. In all instances where food is concerned, do be sure it is fresh and has not been subjected to chemical crop spraying. Wild plants should be gathered from areas away from roadside verges and away from areas that might have been contaminated by dogs.

Guinea pigs, like almost all animals, require water. Clean water should always be available. Watering bottles are available at your local petshop.

Yes, guinea pigs also eat flower petals and succulents. Many plants are poisonous but your cavy knows not to eat those plants in enough quantity to injure themselves.

Above: Rabbits and guinea pigs eat the same things, but guinea pigs (cavies) require certain vitamins in their diets which rabbits can produce by themselves.

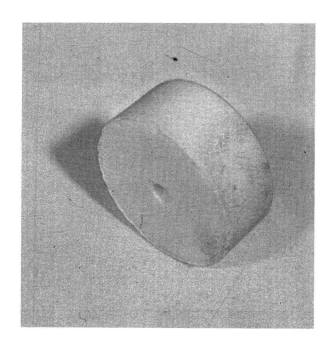

Mineral blocks for rabbits and cavies are available at your local petshop. They should always be available for your pet cavy.

Mashes

To prepare a mash, mix a number of ingredients together, using oats or bran as the base. Be sure all the added items are crushed or crumbled. Next add just enough warm water to soak the mix and hold it together. A mash will quickly sour so do not leave it too long.

You can offer your guinea pig soft mashes which can be stored in a frozen state immediately after being made.

Feeding Routine

It is best to establish a fixed routine when feeding any pets. In this way they will come to expect their food at a given time and will eagerly be waiting to see what is on that meal's menu. Guinea pigs will give out their characteristic little squeal as they see you approaching with the food.

Your guinea pig will await your arrival if he knows about the time of day that he will be fed. Many cavies will not eat natural foods like grasses and flowers if they know their feeding time is approaching.

Unfortunately when spring brings flowers, many cavy keepers give the blossoms to their pets. The sudden switch to this new food may cause scours and should be avoided as much as possible. Offer your pet new blossoms in very limited quantities, certainly not more than it can eat in three minutes.

In the morning give them their ration of greens, fruits and other softfoods. Mashes can be given in the late afternoon when the sun has lost its peak power, so the mash will not sour as quickly as if given earlier in the day. Dryfoods can be given on a more or less ad lib basis so there is always something for the guinea pigs to eat. They have evolved to eat steadily over a period rather than to gorge on a single meal, as do predatory animals.

You will find they will quickly sift through the softfoods to pick out their favorite items, which will be eaten first. You should always watch your pets eat because in this way you get to know their individual preferences and habits. Some are greedy eaters, others only nibble at this or that. When one is not eating as it should, this gives you the first warning sign that something may be amiss. You will soon know how much to

feed by gauging what is left. If they clear the food up in a matter of minutes then you are not giving them enough. They should gain weight steadily and their fur should have a high gloss look to it.

In order to avoid the problem known as scours, never supply a new greenfood suddenly and in quantity. In the spring, wild plants become available and often owners suddenly start

This beautiful cavy has never seen a flower before. It might take 30 minutes for the guinea pig to eat the flower and it would almost certainly become ill.

to give their pets large quantities. The result is diarrhea and other problems. This can largely be avoided by supplying small amounts on a build-up basis. Likewise, start to reduce the quantities as the fall approaches. This applies to all foods that are seasonal in availability.

This albino cavy might have had black markings where the red markings occur, under normal circumstances. But with special coloring foods, albinos can be made to appear tinted like the one shown here.

It is more important to get a healthy guinea pig than a pretty one. The color has little to do with the pet quality. Unless you are interested in breeding cavies, get an animal which is most friendly. The two color varieties shown on this page include the Dalmatian shown above and a tri-color shown below.

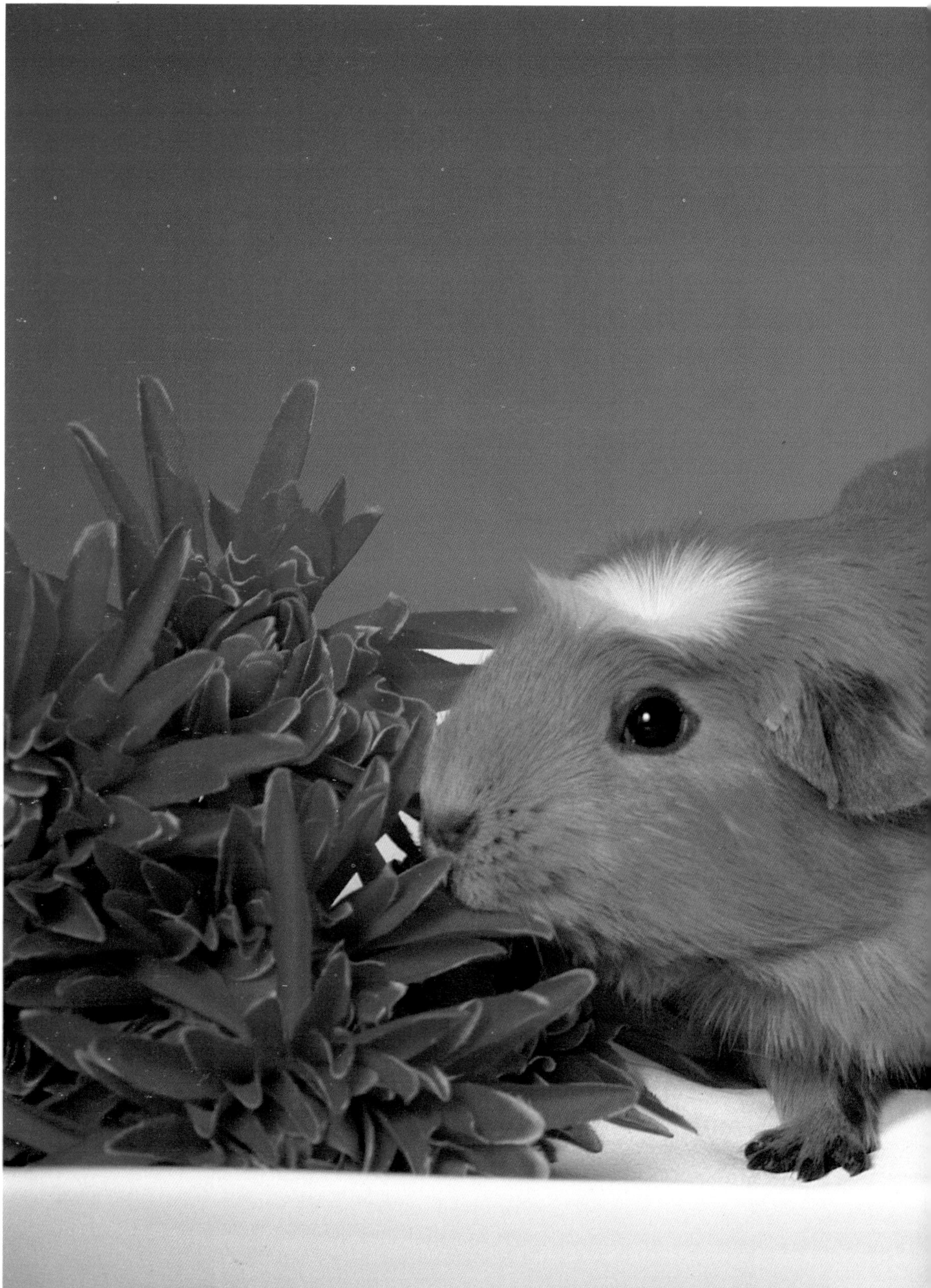

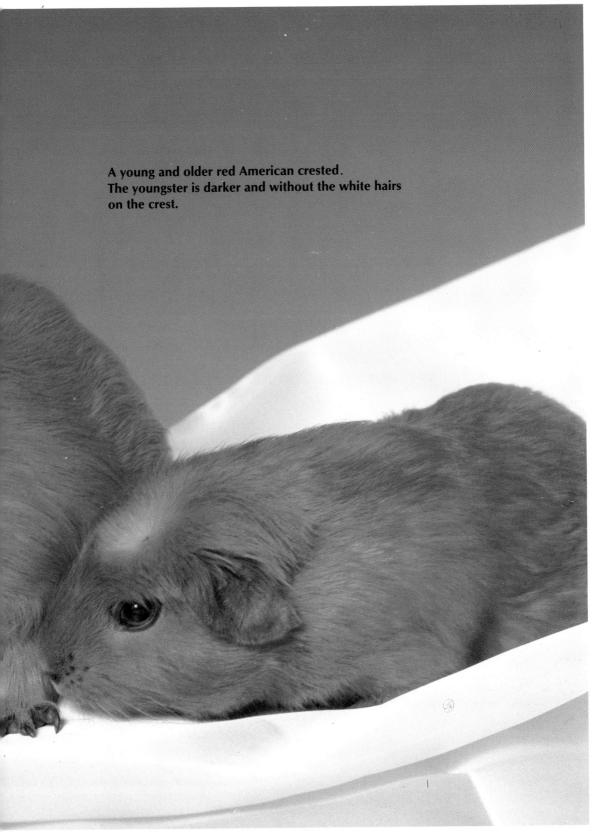

A young and older red American crested.
The youngster is darker and without the white hairs
on the crest.

Supplements

There are many multivitamin supplements marketed for pets these days but use these with care and preferably only under veterinary advice. If a well-balanced diet is supplied, the use of supplements has no benefit whatsoever and could even be dangerous. The interaction of vitamins and minerals is a delicate balance. An excess of one can lead to lack of absorption of another, so only use concentrated powders if you are quite sure something is lacking—in which case you will need veterinary advice first anyway. The more varied the diet supplied the less chance there is that anything will be lacking.

Finally, do remember that water is an essential of life. Even though your guinea pig may obtain much of its needs from the greenfood supplied, it must still have water available to it at all times—and it must be fresh daily.

These two lovely albino cavies are also called *self whites*, or even *Siamese sealpoints* because they have the same darker noses and ears as a Siamese cat.

Breeding

Breeding is a fascinating aspect of keeping guinea pigs, but it will require both time and money. Further, there is little benefit from breeding with other than purebred stock which is of at least a very sound standard. The object is obviously to steadily improve on one's stock by a selective management program that is a continuum. It will cost as much to breed and keep inferior and non-variety stock as it will purebreds, yet the demand and price obtained for surplus stock of the latter will obviously be much higher.

This sow gave birth to this self white. Unless you know the genetic makeup of the parents, you will not be able to predict the probabilities of the color or coat type of the offspring. The mink-like guinea pig on the facing page could have been the sire of the self white.

This red-eyed, long-haired cavy will, if bred with another red-eyed, long-haired cavy produce 100% red-eyed, long-haired cavies.

With these facts in mind it behooves you to both carefully consider which varieties to commence with, and to ensure that you obtain your initial stock from a well-established breeder who can guarantee the purity of its line and thus its genetic makeup.

Additionally, you need stock from a line that has a proven record of breeding vigor—with written records to back this up. You are strongly recommended to learn the basics of genetics; this will make you much more aware how important stock selection is.

These cavies (guinea pigs) are the fifth inbred generation of self-reds. Every one of their offspring will look alike. Because of their hardiness and genetic structure, besides their small size, guinea pigs are favorite laboratory animals and scores of inbred guinea pig varieties are available from petshops and laboratory animal suppliers.

Breeding Facts

The guinea pig is sexually mature at any time after about three months of age. The sow can be bred from at about 4-5 months of age, whilst the boar should ideally be rather older if strong vigorous offspring are to be produced. You could start with just one boar and one sow, but a boar can cover a harem of 3-5 sows if you prefer. Guinea pigs are not prolific breeders like rabbits and the average litter size will be 4-5, though often you may only obtain 1-3. The babies are retained in the sow for about 61-64 days, compared to half this time in rabbits. However, the result is that they are born fully furred, with eyes open and able to run around and feed within hours of their birth.

This cavy is called an *English agouti,* silver phase. It is a genetically engineered variety which was difficult to develop but not worth much in terms of eye-appeal.

Two photos of a tri-colored sow and her tri-colored youngsters. Interestingly, the babies bred true for color, but the offspring have long hair while the sow has rosettes.

The sow's estrus cycle is about every 16 days, so you can leave her with the boar for a number of weeks and during this time she will be mated several times, thus likely to be pregnant. Once you see her gaining weight, especially as she gets near to the birth time, she can be removed to her own quarters. It is possible to colony breed guinea pigs, as often the boar and other sows take great interest and paternal care of all babies, but you can never be sure on this account. Do remember that if the boar is to cover more than one sow, they should all be of the same variety otherwise you will end up with cross varieties.

Once the sow has given birth to a litter she is capable of being mated again, but this has little to recommend it as the likely result will be a loss of vigor in the subsequent youngsters. The sow needs a number of weeks to regain her full physical strength, especially if she is young and thus not fully mature to begin with.

The babies are weaned when they are about 4-5 weeks old and thereafter can live totally independent of their mother. Prior to breeding you should ensure that the sow is given increased amounts of food. This will reduce the likelihood of her experiencing problems created through calcium or other needed ingredient deficiencies. If you have any doubt at all about the health of either potential parent, you should not

Guinea pig sows only have two nipples with which to feed their offspring.

This self-white albino sow was genetically pure, as all albinos are, so the different colored babies are derived from the genes of the father.

During pregnancy, guinea pig sows are extremely delicate and should be handled as carefully and minimally as possible.

Above: A self-red sow with her self-red offspring. Young reds are darker than older ones.

Left:By crossing the self black and the lilac with the red eyes (an albino type), you might get a self black and a self cream...or you might get any genetic makeup of the father, including a self-white albino.

use them at that time for breeding.

The sow guinea pig has only two nipples, so if she has a large litter this clearly makes for a free-for-all at feeding time! However, the fact that the babies can eat solid foods within such a short span of time does greatly help the situation. Nonetheless, if you are presented with a large litter, and

another sow has only a few, it is wise to foster some from one to the other. Do this when the foster mother is preoccupied with eating favored morsels. Wipe your hands over her and her babies and then rub the other youngsters before putting them in with the foster mother's offspring; usually there is no rejection.

Sexing

Guinea pigs are not the easiest of pets to sex, but this is done in the following manner. Lay the guinea pig on its back in your hand. By pressing the genital orifice gently on each side, the penis of the male will protrude. If there is no penis then obviously it is a female. Your pet dealer or breeder supplying the guinea pig will show you how to do this. The guinea pig will need to be old enough for accurate sexing.

Cavies (guinea pigs) mating. Guinea pigs may mate frequently. Their contact is fairly short when compared to dogs.

Facing page: Some people can look at a guinea pig from a distance and tell the sex. Most people cannot do this with any certainty. By pressing the genital orifice, it is possible to positively make a sexual determination.

Record Keeping

It is always worthwhile keeping detailed records of all of your breeding results. These should include information on the sow and boar used, how many babies these produced, the colors and markings of the offspring, their birth and ultimate weight and also any that died and why, if this can be ascertained.

It is impossible to breed cavies on a commercial basis without a knowledge of genetics and a system of record keeping. The basis of record keeping is to identify each breeding animal. This is usually done with a marker attached to the cavy's ear.

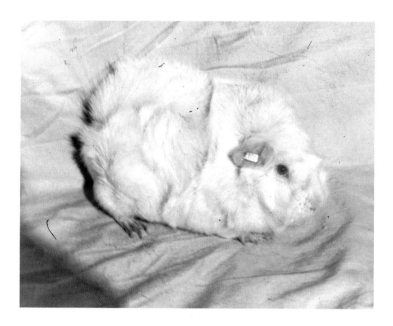

This collective information will prove of importance as your breeding line develops. Once you are satisfied that you are making progress in terms of the overall quality of your stock, you should then try to avoid introducing new bloodlines and concentrate on establishing pureness for given features in your stock. When outside lines are used you cannot be sure what negatives these will bring with them, so if used this must be done under a carefully planned testing program.

It can take years to develop a good stud, and it can easily be undone by using an apparently super boar on your sows. Once you have a nice line of guinea pigs you will find much satisfaction in your efforts, and it will be more in demand than if you practice casual breeding where the 'type' is very variable.

Children handling cavies with markers in their ears should be warned not to disturb the markers as this may cause pain for the cavy and result in a bite or a leap out of their hands.

There are cavies and there are cavies. The animal above is a much higher quality than the animal below...but only in terms of some false standards that were established years ago for exhibition purposes. The only difference between these two animals is their adherence to artificial standards. As far as their quality as pets is concerned, it is quite possible that the lower cavy is a better pet than the cavy shown above.

Exhibition

If you are a breeder, exhibiting your stock is the logical conclusion to your program. It not only enables you to see how it compares with that of other breeders but also provides a selling window for your surplus stock. Further, at shows you will meet many new friends, all of whom share your interest in guinea pigs. Even if you do not breed you can still exhibit your pet in classes specially for these, but obviously there is not quite the same continuation as with those who always have fresh youngsters to campaign.

These are exhibition quality guinea pigs. They are a far cry from the wild guinea pigs found in South America. This photo was actually taken at an exhibition. Let's hope that breeding guinea pigs to a standard does not reduce the pet quality of guinea pigs as it has done in dogs. No part of the standard refers to pet qualities...only physical qualities.

Your first step is to join a local club. This will enable you to compete in table shows. These are informal affairs where there is no benching (penning) provided and each exhibitor keeps their stock in their own carrying boxes. At such events, breeders have more time to talk to you and everything is at a lower key than at the bigger, more competitive, events.

If you find this side of the hobby is to your liking, then the next stage is to visit larger shows, maybe with an exhibitor friend. You will see how everything is organized and will find out what you have

The photos above and on the facing page were taken at a guinea pig show. The judge, with the white coat, handles each animal in order to examine it more thoroughly.

to do to enter future shows. Classes are scheduled based on varieties, and the larger the show the more classes will be available. Some shows are held in conjunction with rabbit exhibitions, others may be devoted solely to guinea pigs.

You will need to join the national cavy association of your country, which will supply details of the regulations that apply to shows held under its rules. If you only have a pet guinea pig of no specific variety, you can still enter shows in the pet classes. These are often restricted to juvenile exhibitors.

Showing your pets is not a profitable business. Indeed, it can be quite expensive if you become 'hooked' on it, but it is a very rewarding area of the hobby. Many owners and breeders do not exhibit but regularly attend shows so they can keep their eye on developments. They may use them as a source of obtaining fresh stock, or just keeping in touch with other breeders.

Regardless of its pedigree, a sick cavy is a problem. No small book like this one can teach you in the identification and treatment of guinea pig diseases. The book can only help you to prevent diseases from occurring.

Health Care

As with any animal, guinea pigs can fall ill to a considerable range of ailments and diseases. In such a small volume it is not possible to discuss these so emphasis is focused on prevention. In any case, correct treatment of a disease is totally dependent on accurate diagnosis, which the average hobbyist is unqualified to undertake. A guinea pig can quickly die if it does not receive veterinary attention, so you should be aware of the symptoms of disease.

Some guinea pigs have hair (fur) which changes colors as the animals become older. Black cavies have been known to become gray with age. Usually guinea pigs are darker the younger they are.

Hygiene

The most common cause of disease in small mammals kept as pets is a lack of hygiene in their management. This becomes progressively more important the more pets you keep together. The subject can be viewed from a number of angles.

Many diseases of guinea pigs are caused by handling. Disease organisms can be carried from one animal to another through the hands of the person handling them.

It is not a bad idea to wash the guinea pig and your hands every time you bring a new animal home from a petshop, exhibition or any place where more than one guinea pig exists.

Accommodation. When hutches are poorly constructed or protected, they soon absorb the urine of the inhabitant. This in turn encourages bacterial and viral colonization, as well as providing many sites for parasites to lay their eggs. Crevices are not easily cleaned. If the hutches are exposed to drafts, these will lower the resistance of the guinea pigs. In turn this will make them more susceptible to problems. Be sure your hutch is really well painted or protected on its inner walls and floor, and repaint this routinely each year.

Cleaning. The longer dirt and fecal matter are allowed to remain on the floor of a hutch, the greater the chances it will attract flies, insects and other pathogens. The risk increases as the weather gets warmer. Remove soaked sawdust daily,

Not only must you keep the hutch clean and odorless, you also have to keep the animals clean if they become dirty and matted with droppings. It's as simple as putting the cavy in the sink and washing the dirt away.

The orange-and-white Abyssinian looks like it needs a haircut and shampoo. However, sometimes the white is never pure white and just looks dirty. A cavy only needs a bath if it smells badly. The roughed-up fur is a genetic characteristic and could never be made smooth.

This guinea pig is clean and well groomed. Try to keep your pet animals clean and they will stay healthy.

as well as feces. Thoroughly clean the hutch out as needed but always at least once per week. Do not simply cover soiled sawdust with more sawdust; this merely makes an ideal bed for bacteria to grow in. Feeding and water dishes must be cleaned daily. Those which are cracked or badly scratched should be discarded. Also, be aware that garden refuse, such as heaps of rotting vegetation and grass clippings, are a prime source of problems, especially if they are near your hutches.

Food. A poorly fed guinea pig will have less ability to resist disease than well fed stock. Food that is not fresh may carry disease organisms. Be sure it is obtained from a supplier who keeps it clean and protected from vermin. Wash all vegetable matter before feeding it. Remove all food not eaten within a few hours. Decaying food is an ideal breeding ground for pathogens.

Long-haired breeds can be groomed easily by your children (if you are lucky enough to have them). A small brush, even a toothbrush or a typewriter brush, works very well on guinea pigs.

The variety of colors in guinea pigs is truly amazing. This tri-colored cavy is similarly colored on its belly. The animal below is a self-mahogany and is considered a rare color variety by many keepers.

This smooth-haired cavy is called a *tortoiseshell and white*. It has similar markings on its back.

Inspection

Your guinea pigs should be inspected daily. This will make them easier to handle and thus better pets. Give them a good check over, especially looking for abrasions on the skin. Such places are a prime means of bacteria gaining access to the blood and thus to internal organs. Treat all small cuts with a suitable ointment or powder. Never assume an abrasion is of no importance. If your pet displays any of the following symptoms you should suspect the worst and contact your vet straight away for advice: running nose, weeping eyes, difficulty in breathing, bloodstained feces or urine, bald patches on the skin, or general lethargy.

Were it not for the color on the feet and ears, this would be an albino or self-white as it is often called. The darkened fur on the feet and ears have not earned this color variation any distinction except that it may be a poorly marked Siamese.

Isolation

Once you suspect a problem the guinea pig should be isolated immediately from other animals. If a problem is confirmed by your vet, you should strip the hutch down and clean it in accordance with the vet's advice. Be real sure that any feeding dishes used in the patient's hutch are never used in the hutches of other guinea pigs. It is always best to number the hutches and the dishes so the latter are always used in the same hutch.

This is a nice lilac English cavy. Regardless of their looks, every cavy brought into your hatch must be considered as a health threat and should be isolated for three weeks under observation.

This magnificent self-white has a completely different head profile than the lilac on the facing page.

Handling

Always wash your hands after handling each guinea pig. If one guinea pig is ill it is best to wear disposable surgical gloves when handling it. If you have a number of guinea pigs it is worthwhile always wearing a nylon overall when attending their needs. This will reduce the possibility of disease transfer via your clothes.

Quarantine

Whenever you obtain additional stock it is wise to keep this away from your other stock for at least twenty-one days. If it is incubating any problem, this will usually show within this time period. This aspect is often ignored by fanciers and can have a disastrous effect on your stock. Do not learn the hard way; apply quarantine as soon as you add more guinea pigs.

This Angolan tri-color should have been kept in quarantine for at least three weeks before it is mixed with other cavies in your hutch.

If you buy a group of cavies from the same source, they can be quarantined together. The only problem with this is that should one get sick, all must be treated for the disease.

There have been rumors that if a child has a cold it can be transmitted to the guinea pig pet. This is simply not true. If a child and his pet cavy have a cold at the same time, it is probably pure coincidence.

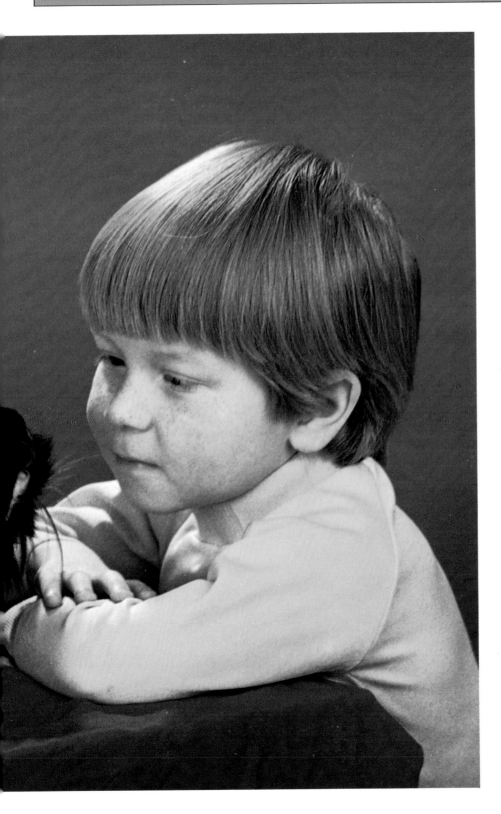

This tri-colored English cavy is of great quality and is typical of those guinea pigs which are available at good petshops.

Which Variety?

There is today a very extensive range of colors, patterns and coat types to be seen in the guinea pig. New varieties are being added all the time as new or recent mutations are transferred to older varieties in order to create new combinations. Further, by selection for what are called modifier genes it is possible to make an existing color darker or paler according to objectives. Any of the existing varieties will make ideal pets, with one notable exception. The longcoated Peruvian, and, to a lesser extent, the more recently developed Sheltie, are not ideal choices for the beginner.

Peruvian or long-haired guinea pigs require a lot of attention and grooming to keep them looking presentable. Keep this in mind if you decide to purchase one or more of them.

The coat of the Peruvian may grow to a length of 51cm(20in) and this can create many problems. It quickly becomes entangled with sawdust, straw or similar material if it is kept on bedding of this type. It may develop the habit of eating its fur—the length of which is in any case an impediment to it. This variety is definitely for the specialist who has the time and inclination to devote to both grooming and wrapping the hairs in paper to keep it neat. It is one of many examples in animals where breeders have taken a feature to extremes purely to satisfy whims of fashion at the expense of the animal carrying the feature.

A nicely marked tortoiseshell and white Peruvian. These only look pretty when they are groomed and the white stays clean.

Self-colored whites or albinos are the most simple animals to breed since all of their offspring will also be albino or self-white.

This lilac self has red eyes which also makes it an albino. Two of the same albinos always breed true to form.

The Basic Varieties

Guinea pigs are divided into two broad groups, these being the self varieties and the non selfs. These divisions can be confusing to the beginner because many cavies in the non self group are in fact self colored—meaning of one color only. The self group comprises all one-color guinea pigs that have a short smooth coat. The non self group includes all other guinea pigs. This means that the Abyssinian and Peruvian varieties, which do not have short smooth coats, are non selfs because of this fact. However, they may be of one color, thus are selfs. Likewise, a guinea pig may have a smooth coat, but because this carries two or three colors it is therefore not a self, thus appears in the non self group.

Guinea pigs, like this one, which have a short coat and a single color are called *selfs*.

This is the original color of cavies from South America. All cavy coat and color variations were derived from animals that looked like this.

The Self Group

The members of this group often, at the highest exhibition level, excel in their body type, as well as in their color. Their heads should be massive, their eyes bold, round and bright. The ears are petal shaped and pendant, showing no signs of damage—such as small tears. The coat is sleek and lustrous whilst the body is muscular and cobby. Producing a top self is not easy because maintaining good coat and color, as well as superb conformation, is a very difficult combination. Of course, this equally applies to most varieties, but possibly in the selfs the standard is now so high that any small failing is enough to put an exhibitor out of contention for prizes.

Self Colors

As in many pets the self black is one of the most difficult colors to produce to a high standard yet is one of the most striking when this is achieved. It is jet black with no trace of red in it (or white hairs). At the opposite extreme the albino is a pure white variety with pink eyes. Actually, it is not an albino in the usual sense but is, genetically speaking, a colorless Himalayan. There is a dark-eyed white but this invariably shows some color in its fur, and some loss of 'type,' so the albino is usually the better proposition.

The self red should be of a mahogany color with no white in it at all. Its eyes are red. It is not as popular as it was some years ago. The self golden is lighter than the red, and there is quite a lot of shade variation seen in this color; it may have pink or dark eyes. The self cream is a nice color, but with any light-colored guinea pig you must be careful that its bedding does not stain its coat. The self buff is a more recent color that is somewhat darker than the cream - and very attractive too. Always a popular choice is the self beige, which looks rather similar to the self lilac, both having pink eyes.

The self chocolate is a color that you either like or dislike. It is very dark and the eyes and ears should match the body color. There is now a self blue, with matching blue eyes.

Lilac English cavy.

Red English cavy.

A tri-colored English cavy.

The Non Self Group

There are many really beautiful smooth-coated guinea pigs in this group, and they carry two or three colors. Possibly the least striking are the agoutis. This is the natural wild color of many animals, including the guinea pig. The hairs are banded in black, brown and yellow to create the familiar ticked pattern. There are golden, silver, cinnamon, lemon and orange agoutis, each having its own devotees.

Chocolate-and-white Peruvian cavy.

Orange Peruvian cavy.

The Dutch variety is always popular and also a difficult pattern to breed to a high standard. The front part of the body is white, there is a white blaze on the face, and the feet are white. The rest of the fur is colored—being either black, or red, or any of a number of other colors. When you breed the Dutch pattern—in guinea pigs, rabbits, or mice— be prepared for the fact that most offspring will be mismarked examples.

A really beautiful variety is the tortoiseshell and white, which is another variety that is very difficult to produce to a high standard. However, any of this variety usually look nice. The colors are black, red and white. The tortoiseshell (brindle) variety is not as popular as a pet. Most people are aware of the Himalayan pattern, which is a variety with dark extremities on a white body. The ears, smut, and feet are either black or chocolate. This is a thermosensitive color so will fade as the

weather gets warmer. This so, most breeders keep their stock indoors during hot periods.

The dappled roans and Dalmatian are a relatively recent addition to the varieties. Roans, as in dogs, are a mixture of colored hairs and white ones, with the head, ears, and feet being colored. The blue dapple is very attractive if the dappled effect of this pattern is good. The Dalmatian is roan where the area of white is extensive, reducing the dapple effect to spots. For breeding success, Dalmatians and roans should be bred as separate lines.

Guinea pigs as pets, laboratory animals or animals to breed for profit, are ideal since they are available in such a variety of colors and fur qualities.

more commonly called the strawberry roan. The magpie is a variation on the roan in that it combines roan with bands of white. The harlequin is a banded bicolor.

The Abyssinian is a fascinating variety because its fur is made up of a series of rosettes and ridges. The fur is quite harsh and the placement of the rosettes is critical in a high quality example. There should be no flat areas of fur in this variety. You can have all of the usual colors, but selfs do not seem to have quite such coarse coats so they are less popular as exhibition animals. The variety also has a reputation for being more prone to biting than do the smooth coats, but this will depend much on how well bred the guinea pig is and how it is handled.

Further, neither should be bred to their own kind but to their own color. The roan mutation, as a homozygote, effects vision, so a black roan should be mated to a black, which will give 50% roans and 50% blacks. Dappled roans are thus what are termed heterozygotes—non purebreeding if problems are to be avoided.

The evenly marked roans are the result of a silvering mutation, which is a different situation to the dappled roans. These can be bred together. The most popular forms are the blue, which is black and silver, and the red, red and silver, which is

Do visit at least your local guinea pig exhibitions. In this way you will get to see most varieties. Until you have seen these you might be missing out on one that would really appeal to you.

Distributed in the UNITED STATES by T.F.H. Publications, Inc., One T.F.H.
Plaza, Neptune City, NJ 07753; in CANADA to the Pet Trade by H & L Pet
Supplies Inc., 27 Kingston Crescent, Kitchener, Ontario N2B 2T6; Rolf C.
Hagen Ltd., 3225 Sartelon Street, Montreal 382 Quebec; in CANADA to the
Book Trade by Macmillan of Canada (A Division of Canada Publishing
Corporation), 164 Commander Boulevard, Agincourt, Ontario M1S 3C7; in
ENGLAND by T.F.H. Publications, PO Box 15, Waterlooville PO7 6BQ; in
AUSTRALIA AND THE SOUTH PACIFIC by T.F.H. (Australia) Pty. Ltd., Box
149, Brookvale 2100 N.S.W., Australia; in NEW ZEALAND by Ross Haines
& Son, Ltd., 82 D Elizabeth Knox Place, Panmure, Auckland, New Zealand;
in the PHILIPPINES by Bio-Research, 5 Lippay Street, San Lorenzo Village,
Makati, Rizal; in SOUTH AFRICA by Multipet Pty. Ltd., P.O. Box 35347,
Northway, 4065, South Africa. Published by T.F.H. Publications, Inc.
Manufactured in the United States of America by T.F.H. Publications, Inc.